The National Athletic Trainers Association
Board of Certification, Inc.

Role Delineation Study
Third Edition

DISCARD

Prepared by Columbia Assessment Services, Inc.

James P. Henderson, PhD
Psychometrician

Steve Heavner
Editor

TABLE OF CONTENTS

ROLE DELINEATION PANEL
DECEMBER 9-11, 1993

Lesa R. Ahrenstein, MA, ATC
3456 Castle Glen Drive #271
San Diego, CA   92123

Gay L. Anderson, MS, LATC
Northeastern University
Lane Health Center
135 Forsyth Building
Boston, MA   02115

Bobby Barton, MS, DA, ATC
Eastern Kentucky University
Alumni Coliseum #128
Richmond, KY   40475

Deborah Cagle, MS, ATC
Salem Hospital-Sports Medicine
P.O. Box 14001
Salem, OR   97309

Robert W. Carmichael, MA, ATC/R
Southwest Missouri State University
901 South National
Springfield, MO   65804

Eva J. Clifton, MS, ATC
Eastern Kentucky University
Alumni Coliseum #129
Richmond, KY   40475

Susan Decker, MS, ATC
Precision Biomechanics, Inc.
5638 Hollister Ave, Suite 304
Goleta, CA   93117

Monica J. Deutsch, MS, ATC
Dodge Physical Fitness Center
Columbia University
New York, NY   10027

Susan Foreman, MEd, ATC, MPT
University of Virginia
P.O. Box 3785
Charlottesville, VA   22903

James D. Gossett, MS, ATC
Columbia University - Nevis Labs
P.O. Box 137
Irvington, NY   10533-0137

Katie Grove, PhD, ATC
Indiana University
Sports Medicine Department
Assembly Hall
Bloomington, IN   47405

Gary W. Lake, MEd, ATC
Summa Health Systems Sports Medicine
600 E. Cuyahoga Falls Avenue
Akron, OH   44310

D. Scott Linaker, MS, ATC
Canyon Del Oro High School
25 W. Calle Concordia
Tucson, AZ   85737

Scot D. McClure, MS, ATC, LAT
Coppell High School
185 W. Parkway Boulevard
Coppell, TX   75019

Kevin Moser, MS, ATC
Kentucky Sports Medicine
601 Perimeter Drive, Suite 200
Lexington, KY   40517

David Regier, MA, ATC
Fort Worth Progress. Rehab. Center, Inc.
3615 Camp Bowie Boulevard
Fort Worth, TX   76107

José E. Rivera, MS, ATC
Center for Sports Medicine
University of Pittsburgh Medical Center
Pittsburgh, PA   15213

Ed Seiler, MA, ATC, MBA
Step 1 Management
P.O. Box 13195
Denver, CO   80201

René Revis Shingles, MS, ATC
Central Michigan University
Dept. of Physical Education/Sport
Rose 133-B
Mt. Pleasant, MI   48859

Chad A. Starkey, PhD, ATC
79 Myrtle Street #1
Watertown, MA   02172

Kim Terrell, MS, ATC
University of Oregon
2727 Leo Harris Parkway
Eugene, OR   97401

Bill Wissen, MA, ATC, LAT
Alief Hastings High School
P.O. Box 68
Alief, TX   77411-0068

ROLE DELINEATION PANEL
DECEMBER 9-11, 1993

Lesa R. Ahrenstein, MA, ATC
3456 Castle Glen Drive #271
San Diego, CA   92123

Gay L. Anderson, MS, LATC
Northeastern University
Lane Health Center
135 Forsyth Building
Boston, MA   02115

Bobby Barton, MS, DA, ATC
Eastern Kentucky University
Alumni Coliseum #128
Richmond, KY   40475

Deborah Cagle, MS, ATC
Salem Hospital-Sports Medicine
P.O. Box 14001
Salem, OR   97309

Robert W. Carmichael, MA, ATC/R
Southwest Missouri State University
901 South National
Springfield, MO   65804

Eva J. Clifton, MS, ATC
Eastern Kentucky University
Alumni Coliseum #129
Richmond, KY   40475

Susan Decker, MS, ATC
Precision Biomechanics, Inc.
5638 Hollister Ave, Suite 304
Goleta, CA   93117

Monica J. Deutsch, MS, ATC
Dodge Physical Fitness Center
Columbia University
New York, NY   10027

Susan Foreman, MEd, ATC, MPT
University of Virginia
P.O. Box 3785
Charlottesville, VA   22903

James D. Gossett, MS, ATC
Columbia University - Nevis Labs
P.O. Box 137
Irvington, NY   10533-0137

Katie Grove, PhD, ATC
Indiana University
Sports Medicine Department
Assembly Hall
Bloomington, IN   47405

Gary W. Lake, MEd, ATC
Summa Health Systems Sports Medicine
600 E. Cuyahoga Falls Avenue
Akron, OH   44310

D. Scott Linaker, MS, ATC
Canyon Del Oro High School
25 W. Calle Concordia
Tucson, AZ   85737

Scot D. McClure, MS, ATC, LAT
Coppell High School
185 W. Parkway Boulevard
Coppell, TX   75019

Kevin Moser, MS, ATC
Kentucky Sports Medicine
601 Perimeter Drive, Suite 200
Lexington, KY   40517

David Regier, MA, ATC
Fort Worth Progress. Rehab. Center, Inc.
3615 Camp Bowie Boulevard
Fort Worth, TX   76107

José E. Rivera, MS, ATC
Center for Sports Medicine
University of Pittsburgh Medical Center
Pittsburgh, PA   15213

Ed Seiler, MA, ATC, MBA
Step 1 Management
P.O. Box 13195
Denver, CO   80201

René Revis Shingles, MS, ATC
Central Michigan University
Dept. of Physical Education/Sport
Rose 133-B
Mt. Pleasant, MI   48859

Chad A. Starkey, PhD, ATC
79 Myrtle Street #1
Watertown, MA   02172

Kim Terrell, MS, ATC
University of Oregon
2727 Leo Harris Parkway
Eugene, OR   97401

Bill Wissen, MA, ATC, LAT
Alief Hastings High School
P.O. Box 68
Alief, TX   77411-0068

TABLE OF CONTENTS

PREFACE

In 1993, the National Athletic Trainers Association Board of Certification (NATABOC), assisted by Columbia Assessment Services, Inc. (CAS), conducted a role delineation study to identify the primary tasks performed by the entry-level athletic trainer. The primary purpose of this study was to establish and validate appropriate content areas for the NATABOC certification examination. The *Role Delineation Study* provides a comprehensive analysis of the work that athletic trainers perform. The NATABOC validated this analysis by collecting specific information from newly credentialed athletic trainers as well as from experienced professionals. Entry into certified status indicates that the ATC is qualified to perform all of the duties described in the Role Delineation Study.

The role delineation study is an integral part of ensuring that an examination is content-valid—that the aspects of the athletic training profession which are covered on the examination are reflective of the tasks performed in an actual practice setting. The study focused on which tasks are performed on the job, how important the tasks are, how frequently the tasks are performed, and how critical the tasks are.

The role delineation study consisted of the following stages:

A. The NATABOC role delineation panel's development of the major content areas (domains) essential to the performance of an entry-level athletic trainer.

B. The panel's development of tasks, knowledge, and skills inherent in the domains previously defined.

C. The development of a pilot study to gather consensus on the panel's role delineation work.

D. An independent review and validation of the panel's domains, tasks, knowledge, and skills by a national sample of NATABOC certified athletic trainers.

This report lists the results of the NATABOC role delineation process, from conception by the role delineation panel to validation by the national survey respondents and subsequent examination development by CAS.

INTRODUCTION

The development of a quality certification or licensing program goes beyond the writing of questions for an examination. Before an examination is developed, a certifying profession must determine what skills and knowledge are needed to be a competent professional in that field. This determination of competencies is a role delineation or job analysis which serves as a blueprint for examination development. This job analysis also determines the type of examination, such as written or practical, to be developed in order to assess competence.

Because examinations are so widely used to certify, license, and consequently employ individuals, psychometricians must follow certain logically-sound and legally-defensible procedures for developing examinations. These principles and procedures are outlined in manuals, such as *Standards for Educational and Psychological Testing*, published by the American Psychological Association in 1985. CAS adheres to these standards in developing examinations for certification programs.

The most important reason for conducting a role delineation is to ensure a test's content validity. In psychometric terms, validation is the way a test developer documents that the competence to be inferred from a test score is actually measured by the items in that examination. A content-valid examination, then, appropriately evaluates knowledge or abilities required to function as a competent practitioner in the field being tested.

A content-valid examination contains a representative sample of items which measure a skill or knowledge contained in the profession being tested. Content validity is the most commonly applied and accepted validation strategy utilized in establishing certification and licensing programs today.

One of the major functions of the NATABOC certification program is to protect the public from the incompetent practitioner. By selecting a certified athletic trainer (ATC), the public is given assurance that the athletic trainer has met specific criteria designed to ensure that he or she is competent. Consequently, the NATABOC attempts to differentiate between the competent and the incompetent athletic trainer, rather than the "good" athletic trainer and the "superior" athletic trainer. The role delineation panel and subsequent validation participants considered only the entry-level athletic trainer when delineating the profession of athletic training. An entry-level ATC has met the NATABOC eligibility requirements and has demonstrated competence in athletic training within the identified performance domains.

NATABOC Study Guide Update

This insert describes changes that have occurred in the NATABOC certification examination and identifies the effect that the new *Role Delineation Study of the Entry-Level Athletic Trainer* will have on the certification examination's content areas. The information presented in this document supersedes that which is described in the accompanying study guide. Where applicable, the page numbers of these changes are noted.

ROLE DELINEATION

Subsequent to the publication of the second edition of the Study Guide, the NATABOC has conducted its third Role Delineation Study of the Entry-Level Athletic Trainer. The Role Delineation (RD) Study serves as the framework around which the certification examination is constructed. The current RD Study, implemented January 1, 1995, has resulted in changes in the content and structure of the certification examination. These effects include changes in the structure and content of the performance domains and a subsequent adjustment in the number of questions from each domain.

Changes Between the Second and Third Role Delineation

One of the most noticeable changes between the second and third editions of the Role Delineation Study is found in the number of performance domains. The previous edition of the Role Delineation Study identified six performance domains **whereas the new Role Delineation Study identifies five** (Table 1).

At first glance, it may appear that the scope of athletic training knowledge has been reduced, it has in fact been expanded by adding to the number of content areas forming each performance domain. A synopsis of the changes between the old and new Role Delineation Studies includes:

- The tasks that were previously identified in "recognition and evaluation of athletic injuries" and "management, treatment, and disposition of athletic injuries" have been absorbed in the current "recognition, evaluation, and immediate care of athletic injuries" and "rehabilitation and reconditioning of athletic injuries" domains.
- "Organization and administration of athletic training programs" has been expanded and reclassified as "health care administration."
- The content area of "education and counseling" has been re-emphasized as a universal competency.
- A new domain, "professional development and responsibility" has been added to the current Role Delineation Study.
- "Universal competencies," a new group of knowledges and skills, have been identified.

1

Table 1. COMPARISON OF THE PERFORMANCE DOMAINS
IDENTIFIED IN THE SECOND AND THIRD EDITIONS OF THE ROLE
DELINEATION STUDY OF THE ENTRY-LEVEL ATHLETIC TRAINER

Second Edition	*Third Edition*
Prevention of athletic injuries	Prevention of athletic injuries
Recognition and evaluation of athletic injuries	Recognition, evaluation, and immediate care of athletic injuries
Management, treatment, and disposition of athletic injuries and illnesses	Rehabilitation and reconditioning of athletic injuries
Rehabilitation of athletic injuries	Health care administration
Organization and administration of athletic training programs	Professional development and responsibility
Education and counseling	

A final important change to note is in the population that athletic trainers service. A significant percentage of athletic trainers responding to the Role Delineation Study survey indicated that they not only provide service to "traditional" athletes, but also that their scope of practice has expanded to include those individuals who meet the definition of nontraditional (i.e., older or younger athletes and athletes with special needs). The group of certified athletic trainers termed this population "physically active individuals."

The Role Delineation Matrix

The revised role delineation identified five major performance domains and 10 universal competencies. The five performance domains define the major areas of practice for athletic trainers. While developing the content areas for each performance domain, it became apparent that certain bodies of knowledge (subject areas) appeared in most, if not all, of the performance domains.

Although each performance domain has its own body of unique knowledges and skills, some subject matter consistently appeared across all domains. These overlapping areas have been termed **universal competencies.** The interrelationship between the performance domains and the universal competencies forms a mosaic, the role delineation matrix, which defines the educational construct of athletic training (Table 2).

To explain the concept of universal competencies, consider "athletic training evaluation." Knowledge of evaluation skills is not limited to the assessment of an acute injury. Athletic trainers are also required to identify the presence of predisposing conditions (**prevention**) and follow-up evaluations used to assess the stage of healing and the efficacy of the treatment and rehabilitation program (**rehabilitation and reconditioning**). Furthermore, the athletic trainer must be able to sufficiently document these findings (**health care administration**) and fulfill an obligation to remain up-to-date with current evaluation skills, knowledge, and techniques (**professional development and responsibility**).

Table 2. TABLE OF UNIVERSAL COMPETENCIES

Universal Competencies / Domain-Specific Content	Prevention of Athletic Injuries	Performance Domains			
		Recognition, Evaluation, and Immediate Care of Athletic Injuries	Rehabilitation and Reconditioning of Athletic Injuries	Health Care Administration	Professional Development and Responsibility
		Knowledge and skills particular to each performance domain			
Athletic Training Evaluation	Determination of an athlete's physical readiness to participate.	Identification of underlying trauma.	Ongoing evaluation of an athlete's progress through various stages of rehabilitation.	Documentation of injury status and rehabilitation.	Remains up-to-date with current evaluation skills, techniques and knowledge.
Human Anatomy	Normal anatomical structure and function.	Recognition of signs and symptoms of athletic injury and illness.	Normal anatomical structure and function.		Remains up-to-date in current human anatomical research and trends.
Human Physiology	Normal physiological function.	Recognition of signs and symptoms of athletic injury and illness.	Stages of injury response.		Remains up-to-date in current human physiology research and trends.
Exercise Physiology	Physiological demand and response to exercise.	Recognition of systemic and local metabolic failure.	Musculoskeletal and cardiovascular demands placed on the injured athlete.		Remains up-to-date with current exercise physiology research and trends.
Biomechanics	Normal biomechanical demands of exercise.	Identification of pathomechanics.	Resolution of pathomechanical motion.		Remains up-to-date with current biomechanical research and trends.
Psychology/Counseling	Educational program for the healthy and injured athlete (i.e., alcohol and other drug abuse, performance anxiety).	Recognition of the psychological signs and symptoms of athletic injury and illness.	Psychological implications of injury.	Communication with, and referral to, the appropriate health care provider.	Continues to develop interpersonal and communication skills.
Nutrition	Nutritional demands of the athlete.	Recognition of the effects of improper nutritional needs of the competing athlete (i.e., fluid replacement, diabetic shock).	Nutritional demands placed on the injured athlete.	Referral to the appropriate health care provider.	Remains up-to-date with current nutritional research and trends.
Pharmacology	Contraindications and side effects of prescription and non-prescription medications.	The role of prescription and non-prescription medication in the immediate/emergency care of athletic injury and illness.	The role of prescription and non-prescription medications in the stages of injury response.	Proper maintenance and documentation of records for the administration of prescription and non-prescription medication.	Remains up-to-date with current pharmacological research and trends.
Physics	Absorption, dissipation, and transmission of energy of varying materials.	The effect of stress loads on the human body (i.e., shear, tensile, compressive forces).	Physiological response to various energies imposed on the body.		Remains up-to-date with current knowledge of physics as it relates to athletic training.
Organization and Administration	Legal requirements and rules of the sport.	Planning, documentation, and communication of appropriate rehabilitation strategies to the necessary parties.	Planning, documentation, and communication of appropriate rehabilitation strategies to the necessary parties.	Development of operational policies and procedures.	Remains up-to-date with current standards of professional practice.

Table 3. DISTRIBUTION OF WRITTEN QUESTIONS BY DOMAINS
IDENTIFIED BY THE ROLE DELINEATION STUDY

Performance Domain	Number of Questions
Prevention of athletic injuries	31
Recognition, evaluation, and immediate care of athletic injuries	59
Rehabilitation and reconditioning of athletic injuries	42
Health care administration	9
Professional development and responsibility	9
Total	150

Examination Changes

The importance, criticality, and frequency of each task in the Role Delineation Study are used to create the specifications for the written examination. Based on these criteria, the number of questions from each performance domain on the written examination is presented in Table 3. This table replaces Table 2 (page 7) in the Study Guide.

The written simulation and practical examination have no requirement for the number of questions per domain. However, when preparing for the practical examination the candidate must pay close attention to all psychomotor skill areas identified in the Role Delineation Study. Changes in the practical examination are discussed in the following section. **No changes have occurred in the written simulation section of the certification examination,** but the candidate must be mindful of the new content areas identified in the third edition of the Role Delineation Study.

Where to Obtain More Information

The third edition of the *Role Delineation Study of the Entry-Level Athletic Trainer* may be ordered from the F.A. Davis Company (800-523-4049).

PRACTICAL EXAMINATION

The description presented in this revision updates the description of the practical examination presented on pages 13 through 15 of the Study Guide. The practical examination has been modified so that it now focuses only on the performance of specific psychomotor skills. Candidates are asked to perform a series of specific skills and the examiner evaluates each problem according to the component tasks necessary to complete the skill. Examples of the tasks that the candidate may be asked to perform include, but are not limited to:

Ambulation assists
Ligamentous stress tests
Manual muscle tests

Protective device construction
Reflex testing
Sensory testing
Special tests
Taping and Wrapping
Vital signs

The practical examination no longer has scenario-type situations such as "An athlete complains of knee pain . . .", a revision that eliminates traditional candidate responses such as, "I would ask the athlete where the pain is located" because it is not a psychomotor skill. Rather, the candidate will be given such tasks to perform such as, "Please demonstrate how you would perform manual muscle tests for knee flexion and extension. You have 3 minutes to complete your response." The candidate should expect to encounter 8 to 14 such tasks per examination.

Referring to the sample oral/practical examination questions on pages 105 and 106 of the study guide, the new format for this section would most closely resemble problem 2 than problem 1. You will not that responses 9 through 15 all relate to the physical skills required to properly fit an athlete with a pair of crutches and teach the athlete how to walk with them. Responses 16 through 19 **would not** appear on the practical examination because there is no psychomotor component. Questions such as sample question 1 have been reworked to eliminate all nonskill-related tasks such as those presented in responses 1, 2, 5, 6, 7, and 8. However, palpation of the abdomen (tasks 3 and 4) **could** appear on the oral/practical examination because they represent evaluations skills.

The actual administration of the practical examination remains the same as in the past. There are still two examiners and a model. Each skill must be performed within a predetermined time frame, usually ranging from 2 to 5 minutes. However, examination guide booklets **will not** be distributed to the candidate as in the past.

PHASE I:
INITIAL DEVELOPMENT AND EVALUATION

The first steps in studying the athletic training profession were the identification of the major task areas or domains, the listing of tasks performed under each domain, and the identification of the knowledges and skills associated with each task. The following steps were undertaken to achieve Phase I:

A. After consultation with CAS, the NATABOC assembled a 20-member panel of subject matter experts in the field of athletic training to discuss the role of the certified athletic trainer. The panel members represented a variety of practice settings and were assembled from different regions of the country.

This panel reviewed the 1989 role delineation study and determined that the profession had evolved significantly in four years. Their discussion focused on the recent turn in the field toward clinical and industrial settings—athletic trainers are working in clinical and industrial settings as well as in the traditional "athletic trainer settings" such as high schools, colleges, and the like.

Thus, panel members discussed the relevance of the term "athlete" as to its definition regarding the recipient of athletic training services. For example, is the 70-year-old who walks a mile three times a week considered an athlete? Maybe not, yet this person may well present to ATCs with injuries or problems. Therefore, the panel members settled on the term "athlete or physically active individual" to encompass a wider audience than was previously considered.

The panel members discussed the role of the athletic trainer as it compares to the role of physical therapists and attempted to differentiate between the two. The panel stressed that the athletic trainer should be responsible for athletic injuries. For example, the athletic trainer should not provide services to the person wanting a back examination in order to sit in a chair more comfortably. Instead, the athletic trainer should focus on the injuries that occur as a result of physical activity. Physical therapists or other medical personnel may supply services for the injuries and complaints of non-athletes.

With these understandings in mind, the panel then determined that the five domains listed on the next page were appropriate for the certified athletic training profession.

Performance Domains
1. Prevention of Athletic Injuries
2. Recognition, Evaluation, and Immediate Care of Athletic Injuries
3. Rehabilitation and Reconditioning of Athletic Injuries
4. Health Care Administration
5. Professional Development and Responsibility

In the process of defining the five performance domains, the panel realized there were certain elements of athletic training that could not be assigned to any singular domain. In fact, these elements "transcend" domains in that they are specific components that may be classified appropriately under several domains. Thus, the panel considered it necessary to include these elements in the task development processes of the domains. For example, the panel considered anatomy to be basic knowledge inherent in all aspects of an athletic trainer's duties and felt that if anatomy were not included in the role delineation in some fashion, then students or interns preparing to become athletic trainers may not receive the necessary building blocks to enable them to become professionals in the field. These transcending content areas, termed universal competencies, which organize the knowledge and skill statements for each task as they are relevant are listed below. See Appendix 1, page 57, for details of the universal competencies.

Universal Competencies
1. Domain-Specific Content
2. Athletic Training Evaluation
3. Human Anatomy
4. Human Physiology
5. Exercise Physiology
6. Biomechanics
7. Psychology/Counseling
8. Nutrition
9. Pharmacology
10. Physics
11. Organization and Administration

B. Keeping in mind the changing role of certified athletic trainers, the panel next directed its attention to the delineation of the tasks in each of the five domains performed by entry-level certified athletic trainers and generated a list of knowledges and skills required to perform each task. During and after the meeting, CAS staff members provided psychometric editing of the task, knowledge, and skill statements.

C. The panel subsequently evaluated each domain and task according to its importance and criticality to the entry-level ATC and to the frequency with which the activities associated with each domain and task are performed. See Appendix 2, page 58, for more information on the rating scales used.

PHASE II:
VALIDATION STUDY

Questionnaire Design and Distribution

CAS staff members developed a 12-page questionnaire and distributed it to 200 experts in the field of athletic training as a pilot study to provide preliminary feedback on the role delineation panel's domain and task list. These returned questionnaires were reviewed and analyzed, with corrections incorporated into the next step of the study—the larger validation survey.

CAS then distributed the updated survey to 2,000 experts in the field of athletic training to evaluate, validate, and provide feedback on the role delineation panel's task list. The survey sample was randomly drawn from a database of certified athletic trainers practicing throughout the country. The questionnaire solicited biographical information from the respondents in order to document their qualifications as subject matter experts. This information helped provide verification that the sample represented all major job functions. Of the 2000 questionnaires mailed out, 810 usable responses were returned to CAS.

Results

As reflected in the biographical data and graphs on the following pages, the survey respondents represent many levels of education and experience. Sixty-one percent of the respondents (491) are male and 39% (317) are female. Forty percent of the respondents (326) have between one and five years of experience in athletic training, with another 25% (202) having between six and 10 years of experience in the field. Most of the respondents (462, or 58%) hold Master's Degrees, while another 27% (220) hold Bachelor's Degrees. Thirty-two percent (255) of the respondents are head athletic trainers. Twenty-eight percent, or 223, of the respondents work in a college or university setting; eighteen percent (147) work in a clinical setting full time, and another 22%, or 173, work in a clinical setting part time. Over half the respondents were certified via the curriculum route, with 49%, or 388 respondents, certified through an undergraduate curriculum and 11%, or 87 respondents, certified through a graduate curriculum. Because not all survey respondents answered all biographical questions, the total number of respondents reflected in the graphs may not equal the total number of surveys returned.

Gender of Survey Respondents

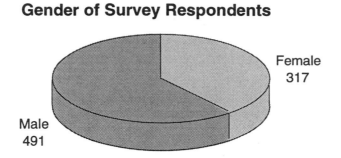

Female 317

Male 491

Educational Level of Respondents

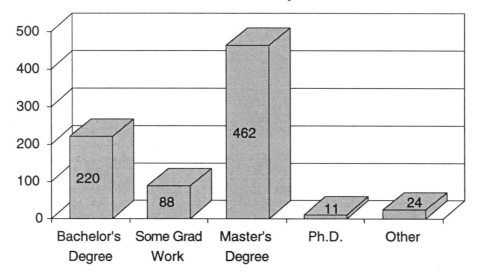

Years of Experience in Athletic Training

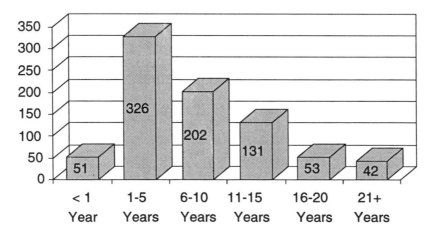

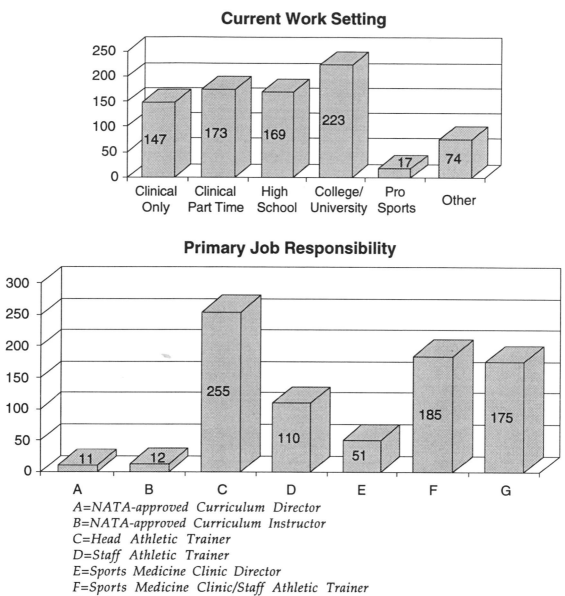

Current Work Setting

Clinical Only	147
Clinical Part Time	173
High School	169
College/University	223
Pro Sports	17
Other	74

Primary Job Responsibility

A	11
B	12
C	255
D	110
E	51
F	185
G	175

A=NATA-approved Curriculum Director
B=NATA-approved Curriculum Instructor
C=Head Athletic Trainer
D=Staff Athletic Trainer
E=Sports Medicine Clinic Director
F=Sports Medicine Clinic/Staff Athletic Trainer
G=Other

Certification Route of Respondents

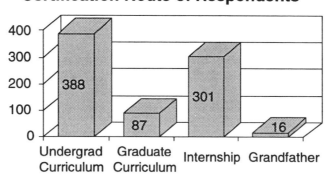

Undergrad Curriculum	388
Graduate Curriculum	87
Internship	301
Grandfather	16

Evaluation of Performance Domains

Survey respondents were asked to evaluate the importance and criticality of the five performance domains, in addition to estimating the amount of time spent performing the duties required within the domains. These survey data were analyzed in two ways: 1) the survey data were compared to the data developed by the role delineation panel and 2) the survey data were analyzed and evaluated by subgroups of the respondents.

A. NATA Role Delineation Panel Data Versus Survey Respondent Data

The evaluations of domains by the role delineation panel were compared to the evaluations of domains by the survey respondents. The results are shown in the following charts. Panel members and survey respondents showed only minor variations in their ratings of domain importance; the most significant difference (less than one rating point) is shown in the two groups' ratings of Domain 4 (Health Care Administration). Regarding domain criticality, again Domain 4 showed the most significant difference in the two groups' ratings, with the panel members rating the domain more critical than the survey respondents did (4.22 to 2.90). The two groups ranked the frequency of the activities performed within the domains similarly, with variances of 6% or less in each case.

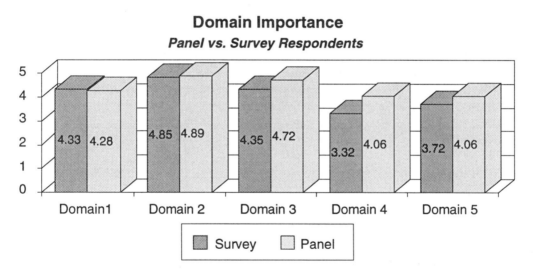

Domain Importance
Panel vs. Survey Respondents

Scale: 1 (not important) to 5 (extremely important)

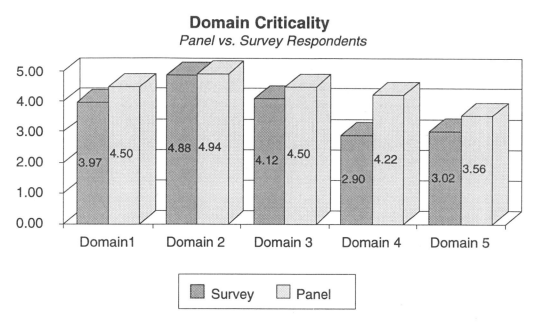

Domain Criticality
Panel vs. Survey Respondents

Scale: 1 (causing no harm) to 5 (causing extreme harm)

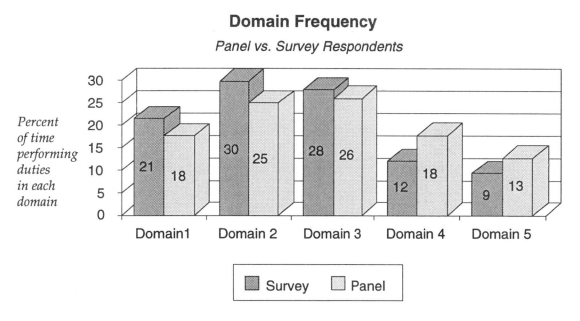

Domain Frequency
Panel vs. Survey Respondents

B. Analysis of Survey Respondent Data

The data collected from subgroups of respondents were analyzed and compared with the data collected from the overall group of respondents. Such a comparison is necessary to ensure that specified subgroups do not view the profession of athletic training differently from the way the majority of respondents view the profession. With this possibility of difference in mind, CAS staff members analyzed the responses of several subgroups, including those of gender, educational level, and years of experience. A summary of this analysis appears in the following tables. As the tables reflect, the various subgroups view the domains and tasks in a manner similar to that of the overall group of respondents.

From an examination of the tables below and on the following page, we can see that the responses of the subgroups identified in the survey all seem to view the domains in approximately the same way. Domain 2 was considered the most important and the most critical of the five domains, followed closely by Domains 1 and 3. Domains 4 and 5 were considered the least important and critical in each of the subgroups. This similarity in ranking provides support for generalizing from the survey results to the population of certified athletic trainers in general. Accordingly, examination specifications were developed based on this data without different content or testing methodologies for certain subgroups.

Domain Importance by Gender

	Domain 1	Domain 2	Domain 3	Domain 4	Domain 5
Female	4.35	4.91	4.46	3.38	3.79
Male	4.32	4.81	4.29	3.28	3.67

Domain Criticality by Gender

	Domain 1	Domain 2	Domain 3	Domain 4	Domain 5
Female	4.01	4.89	4.19	2.94	3.12
Male	3.94	4.87	4.08	2.88	2.96

Domain Importance by Education Level

	Domain 1	Domain 2	Domain 3	Domain 4	Domain 5
Bachelor's	4.24	4.81	4.38	3.28	3.66
Some Grad	4.33	4.93	4.34	3.29	3.78
Master's	4.38	4.87	4.34	3.33	3.73
Ph.D.	4.30	4.80	4.40	3.50	3.60
Other	4.43	4.61	4.39	3.57	3.83

Domain Criticality by Education Level

	Domain 1	Domain 2	Domain 3	Domain 4	Domain 5
Bachelor's	3.62	4.84	3.96	2.95	2.70
Some Grad	3.82	4.89	4.21	2.97	2.92
Master's	3.83	4.89	4.02	3.11	2.85
Ph.D.	4.21	4.82	4.13	3.39	3.03
Other	3.70	4.89	4.02	3.34	3.16

Domain Importance by Experience of Respondent

	Domain 1	Domain 2	Domain 3	Domain 4	Domain 5
< 1 year	4.22	4.84	4.41	3.45	3.96
1-5 years	4.32	4.86	4.35	3.27	3.74
6-10 years	4.35	4.86	4.38	3.29	3.67
11-15 years	4.31	4.85	4.34	3.42	3.65
16-20 years	4.46	4.87	4.27	3.40	3.69
21+ years	4.43	4.73	4.33	3.31	3.73

Domain Criticality by Experience of Respondent

	Domain 1	Domain 2	Domain 3	Domain 4	Domain 5
< 1 year	3.82	4.78	4.10	3.06	3.16
1-5 years	3.98	4.85	4.06	2.86	3.00
6-10 years	3.95	4.93	4.18	2.84	2.97
11-15 years	3.98	4.88	4.16	2.97	3.08
16-20 years	4.00	4.92	4.08	3.00	3.02
21+ years	4.10	4.90	4.35	3.10	3.15

Domain Importance by Work Setting

	Domain 1	Domain 2	Domain 3	Domain 4	Domain 5
Clinical Only	4.15	4.72	4.43	3.15	3.68
Clinical Part Time	4.32	4.89	4.34	3.17	3.77
High School	4.36	4.89	4.28	3.35	3.65
College/ University	4.40	4.91	4.39	3.50	3.71
Pro Sports	4.65	5.00	4.76	3.59	4.06
Other	4.41	4.70	4.18	3.31	3.74

Domain Criticality by Work Setting

	Domain 1	Domain 2	Domain 3	Domain 4	Domain 5
Clinical Only	3.84	4.81	4.19	2.85	2.95
Clinical Part Time	3.90	4.85	4.06	2.78	2.98
High School	3.69	4.89	4.04	2.84	2.96
College/ University	4.07	4.90	4.16	3.06	3.14
Pro Sports	4.00	4.94	4.47	3.47	3.59
Other	4.08	4.96	4.15	2.88	2.96

Summary of Results

As shown in the data below and in the charts on the next page, survey respondents felt that all the domains have a high rating of importance. The domains have an average importance rating of at least 3.32 on the rating scale, with 3 being important and 4 being very important. Domain 2 (Recognition, Evaluation, and Immediate Care of Athletic Injuries) was considered the most important (4.85), followed by Domain 3 (Rehabilitation and Reconditioning of Athletic Injuries, 4.35), Domain 1 (Prevention of Athletic Injuries, 4.33), Domain 5 (Professional Development and Responsibility, 3.72) and Domain 4 (Health Care Administration, 3.32).

The respondents felt the domains follow the same order of criticality as importance. Domain 2 (Recognition, Evaluation, and Immediate Care of Athletic Injuries) was judged to be the most critical with a rating of 4.88, followed by Domain 3 (Rehabilitation and Reconditioning of Athletic Injuries, 4.12) and Domain 1 (Prevention of Athletic Injuries, 3.97). Domain 4 (Health Care Administration) and Domain 5 (Professional Development and Responsibility) were considered less critical, being rated 3.02 and 2.90, respectively, on the rating scale. These similar ratings between importance and criticality reflect the respondents' views that importance and criticality are parallel in the athletic training profession.

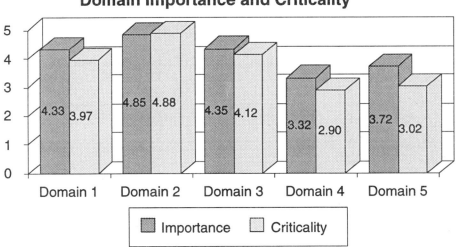

Domain Importance and Criticality

The respondents considered duties of Domain 2 (Recognition, Evaluation, and Immediate Care of Athletic Injuries) to be the most frequently performed, taking up 30% of an entry-level athletic trainer's time. Domain 3 (Rehabilitation and Reconditioning of Athletic Injuries) was next (28%), followed by Domain 1 (Prevention of Athletic Injuries, 21%), Domain 4 (Health Care Administration, 12%), and Domain 5 (Professional Development and Responsibility, 9%).

Domain Frequency

Percent of time performing duties in each domain

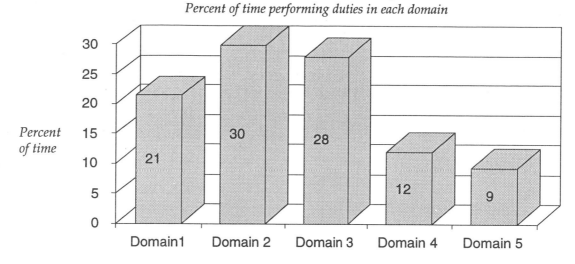

Evaluation of Knowledge and Skills

The next phase of analysis in the role delineation process is a review of the knowledge and skill statements for the purpose of discerning appropriate testing formats. Through this content analysis, knowledge and skill statements are classified into several groups: (a) cognitive understandings, (b) decision-making abilities, and (c) psychomotor skills.

Cognitive understandings in the NATABOC role delineation study include recall of factual information, application of information, analysis of information, and other higher order abilities. Other abilities were found in which entry-level athletic trainers process information on many topics to make and carry out decisions: planning, modifying, interpreting, monitoring, reacting, and revising. Psychomotor skills in the study may be classified as complex, overt responses and adaptation. These are among the highest abilities in the psychomotor domain.

All of the knowledge statements were classified in the cognitive domain. An example of a statement that implies recall of factual information comes from Domain 4, Task 2: "Knowledge of universal precautions required in managing infectious diseases." An example of a knowledge statement implying a higher-order cognitive ability, from Domain 2, Task 1, is "Knowledge of the relationship between predisposing factors and athletic injuries/illnesses."

One of the skills that require athletic trainers to make decisions by interpreting, from Domain 1, Task 3, is "Skill in interpreting data regarding environmental conditions." A decision-making skill that requires the athletic trainer to react, from the same domain and task, is "Skill in implementing and communicating safety guidelines regarding activity in specific environmental conditions."

Finally, other skills fit clearly into the psychomotor domain. Adaptation skills include statements such as Domain 1, Task 5: "Skill in constructing, fabricating, designing, applying, or fitting custom protective devices (e.g., donut pads, splints, orthotics)." From Domain 2, Task 3, is an example of a psychomotor skill classified as a complex, overt response: "Skill in palpating pertinent areas of the body in order to assess integrity of human anatomical/physiological systems (e.g., circulatory, nervous, digestive, lymphatic)."

The psychometric analysis of knowledge and skill statements gives direction to the type of examination formats and problems for the appropriate assessment of competence in athletic training.

PHASE III:
TEST SPECIFICATIONS

The final phase of the NATABOC role delineation is the development of test specifications—the allocation of questions based on each of the domains to be included in the certification examination. The three ratings of domains and tasks—importance, criticality, and frequency—are used to determine the test specifications. Combining these three ratings provides a practical method of taking into account the summative judgments that these three values represent. The values can be converted into percentages, which subsequently are averaged to determine a percentage value for each domain. These percentages are then utilized to determine the number of questions that should appear on a test for each domain. The number of questions coming from each domain based on a 150-item examination is shown in the following chart.

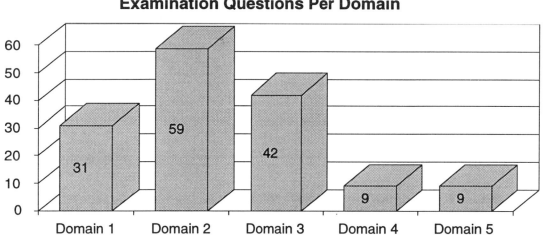

Examination Questions Per Domain

CONCLUSION

From a psychometric analysis of the tasks, knowledges, and skills developed and validated, as well as from an analysis of the data, the examination program should evaluate knowledge and psychomotor skills and decision-making abilities required to assess the competence of athletic trainers. A written examination may be used to assess the knowledges inherent in athletic training. A written simulation, or clinical competency test, is necessary for adequate evaluation of athletic trainers' decision making in typical situations. Finally, the competent performance of skills is basic to the services that athletic trainers provide, and an appropriate measure of skill is essential to the testing program.

In addition to identifying the tasks performed in each performance domain, the role delineation panel also delineated the major knowledge and skills required for the performance of each task. The next section of the report lists the tasks, the survey data relating to each task, and the knowledge and skills required to perform each task. Also included with each domain is the number of questions which should be generated per task for a 150-question examination.

The National Athletic Trainers Association Board of Certification, Inc.

Role Delineation Study

Domain 1. Prevention of Athletic Injuries

Domain 2. Recognition, Evaluation, and Immediate Care of Athletic Injuries

Domain 3. Rehabilitation and Reconditioning of Athletic Injuries

Domain 4. Health Care Administration

Domain 5. Professional Development and Responsibility

Domain 1. Prevention of Athletic Injuries

Task Evaluation

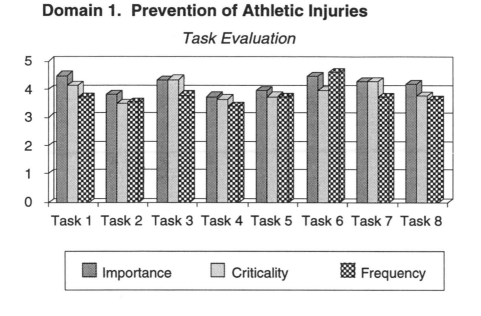

Importance   Criticality   Frequency

Evaluation and Allocation of Questions for Domain 1.

Task #	Importance Average	Criticality Average	Frequency Average	# Questions
1	4.49	4.13	3.71	4
2	3.82	3.48	3.53	3
3	4.33	4.34	3.78	5
4	3.73	3.65	3.40	3
5	3.96	3.74	3.72	3
6	4.45	3.94	4.59	5
7	4.28	4.28	3.70	4
8	4.17	3.75	3.63	4

Total number of questions from this domain on the examination: 31

Domain 1. Prevention of Athletic Injuries

Task 1. Identify physical conditions predisposing the athlete or physically active individual to increased risk of injury/illness in athletic activity by following accepted pre-participation examination guidelines in order to ensure safe participation.

Knowledge of:

Domain-Specific Content
1. Accepted pre-participation examination guidelines.

Athletic Training Evaluation
2. Historical conditions that pre-dispose or increase the risk of injury to the athlete or physically active individual in a specific activity.

3. Present physical findings that pre-dispose or increase the risk of injury to the athlete or physically active individual in a specific activity.

Human Anatomy
4. The body's normal function.

Human Physiology
5. The body's normal function.

Exercise Physiology
6. Anthropometric measures.

Biomechanics
7. Normal structural relationships.

Nutrition
8. Principles of the nutritional demands of the athlete.

Pharmacology
9. Contraindications and side-effects of prescription and non-prescription medication in relation to exercise.

Organization and Administration
10. Guidelines for safe participation (NCAA, American Academy of Pediatrics, etc.).

Skill in:

Athletic Training Evaluation

1. Assisting physicians or health care personnel in administering pre-participation physical examinations (e.g., body fat, pulse, blood pressure).

2. Assisting physicians and/or other health care personnel in determining pre-existing conditions predisposing an athlete to increased risk of injury.

Organization and Administration

3. Organization and administration of pre-participation physical examinations (e.g., preparing proper forms, scheduling physicians, organization of examination site).

Task 2. Supervise conditioning programs and testing for athletes or physically active individuals using mechanical and/or other techniques in order to ensure readiness for safe participation in physical activity.

Knowledge of:

Human Anatomy

1. The body's adaptation to conditioning.

Human Physiology

2. The body's adaptation to conditioning.

Exercise Physiology

3. The body's adaptation to conditioning.

4. Muscular strength testing, minimum requirements for specific physical activity, and training principles and techniques.

5. Muscular endurance testing, minimum requirements for specific physical activity, and training principles and techniques.

6. Cardiovascular endurance testing, minimum requirements for specific physical activity, and training principles and techniques.

7. Body composition testing and accepted ranges.

8. Flexibility testing, minimum requirements, and training principles and techniques.

9. Specific activity requirements for conditioning.

Biomechanics

10. Physical principles governing exercise apparatuses.

Organization and Administration

11. Safety principles as related to conditioning activities.

Skill in:

Domain-Specific Content

1. Organizing, recording, and interpreting muscular strength, muscular endurance, flexibility, cardiovascular, and body composition tests.

2. Designing conditioning programs to meet the individual's or group's needs specific to their activity.

Exercise Physiology

3. Operating equipment utilized in muscular strength, muscular endurance, flexibility, cardiovascular, and body composition assessments.

Organization and Administration

4. Identifying safe use and maintenance of conditioning equipment.

5. Effective communication with the individuals involved with the conditioning program.

Task 3. Monitor environmental conditions (e.g., temperature, humidity, lightning) of playing or practice areas by following accepted guidelines in order to make recommendations regarding safe participation.

Knowledge of:

Domain-Specific Content

1. Accepted guidelines of environmental conditions as they relate to safe participation (e.g., ACSM, US Weather Service, AAP, AAFOF, AMA).

2. Local environmental conditions as they relate to the athlete or physically active individual's participation.

Athletic Training Evaluation

3. Predisposing factors that increase the risk of injury/illness from environmental conditions.

Exercise Physiology

4. Physiological effects of environmental conditions.

5. Specific activity demands in regard to environmental conditions.

Nutrition

6. Proper electrolyte and fluid replacement as it relates to the athlete or physically active individual's specific activity.

Skill in:

Domain-Specific Content

1. Interpreting data regarding environmental conditions.

2. Obtaining data regarding environmental conditions (e.g., sling psychrometer, temperature, humidity, weather information).

Organization and Administration

3. Implementing and communicating safety guidelines regarding activity in specific environmental conditions.

Task 4. Assess athletic apparatuses and athletic activity areas (e.g., playing surfaces, gyms, locker and athletic training room facilities) by periodic inspection and review of maintenance records to ensure a safe environment.

Knowledge of:

Domain-Specific Content

1. What constitutes a hazardous situation in or around athletic facilities (e.g., uneven terrain, damaged equipment)

2. The maintenance process for athletic apparatuses and facilities.

Skill in:

Domain-Specific Content

1. Recognizing hazardous conditions in or around athletic facilities.

2. Implementing procedures to correct hazardous conditions and provide guidelines for safe use of athletic apparatuses and facilities.

Task 5. Construct custom protective devices by fabricating and fitting with appropriate materials in order to protect specific parts of the body from injury during athletic activity.

Knowledge of:

Domain-Specific Content
1. Material selection for custom protective devices.

2. Selecting, designing, fabricating, applying, and fitting custom protective devices.

Human Anatomy
3. Mechanisms of injury involved in specific activities.

Biomechanics
4. Mechanisms of injury involved in specific activities.

Physics
5. Absorption, dissipation, and transmission of energy.

Organization and Administration
6. Specific sport requirements and regulations in regard to the use of custom protective devices.

7. The legal and safety risks involved in the construction of custom protective devices.

Skill in:

Domain-Specific Content
1. Recognizing conditions requiring or benefiting from custom protective devices.

2. Constructing, fabricating, designing, applying, or fitting custom protective devices (e.g., donut pads, splints, orthotics).

Task 6. Apply specific and appropriate taping, wrapping, or prophylactic devices to the athlete or physically active individual by adhering to principles of biomechanics and injury mechanism in order to prevent injury or re-injury.

Knowledge of:

Domain-Specific Content
1. Proper material or product selection for taping, wrapping, or using prophylactic devices.

2. The application and removal techniques for taping, wrapping, or prophylactic devices.

Human Anatomy
3. Mechanisms of injury involved in specific activities.

Biomechanics
4. Mechanisms of injury involved in specific activities.

Organization and Administration
5. Rules and requirements specific to the activity for taping, wrapping, or prophylactic devices.

Skill in:

Domain-Specific Content
1. The selection and application of taping, wrapping, and unwrapping techniques.

2. The selection, fitting, and removal of prophylactic devices.

Task 7. Evaluate the use and maintenance of protective devices and athletic equipment (e.g., helmets, shoulder pads, shin guards) by inspecting and assessing the equipment in order to ensure optimal protection of the athlete or physically active individual.

Knowledge of:

Domain-Specific Content

1. The various types of protective devices and equipment utilized and required for participation (e.g., shoulder pads, helmets, shin guards).

2. The purpose and function of protective devices and equipment used for participation (e.g., mouthguards, shoulder pads, helmets).

3. The proper fit and construction of protective devices and equipment.

4. Current professional standards regarding use and maintenance of protective equipment.

Skill in:

Domain-Specific Content

1. Determining the special needs for protective devices and athletic equipment.

2. Proper selection and fitting of protective devices and equipment.

3. Recognizing and removing defective devices and equipment.

Task 8. Educate parents, staff, coaches, athletes, etc., about the risks associated with participation and unsafe practices using direct communication in order to provide an opportunity for them to make an informed decision concerning physical activity.

Knowledge of:

Domain-Specific Content

1. Unsafe practices associated with participation.

2. Inherent risks which include injury frequency and severity associated with specific activities.

3. Inherent risks associated with predisposing physical conditions of the athlete or physically active individual.

Psychology/Counseling

4. Educational programs for the healthy and injured athlete (e.g., alcohol and other drug abuse, anxiety).

Organization and Administration

5. Communication skills (written and verbal).

Skill in:

Organization and Administration

1. Interpersonal communication in order to make an educated, informed decision concerning physical participation.

2. Documenting the informed decision concerning physical participation.

Domain 2. Recognition, Evaluation, and Immediate Care of Athletic Injuries

Task Evaluation

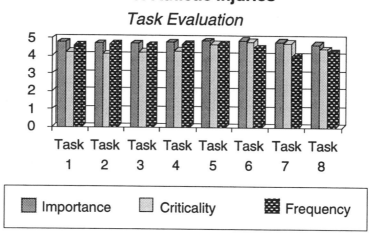

Importance   Criticality   Frequency

Evaluation and Allocation of Questions for Domain 2.

Task #	Importance Average	Criticality Average	Frequency Average	# Questions
1	4.78	4.23	4.62	7
2	4.71	4.11	4.68	7
3	4.70	4.22	4.65	7
4	4.80	4.32	4.66	8
5	4.87	4.66	4.67	8
6	4.91	4.82	4.50	8
7	4.82	4.74	4.00	7
8	4.68	4.4	4.26	7

Total number of questions from this domain on the examination: 59

Domain 2. Recognition, Evaluation, and Immediate Care of Athletic Injuries

Task 1. Obtain a history from the athlete or physically active individual or witnesses through observation and interview in order to determine the pathology and extent of injury/illness.

Knowledge of:

Athletic Training Evaluation
1. Pathomechanics of athletic injury.

2. Relationship between predisposing factors and athletic injuries/illnesses.

3. The body's immediate and delayed physiological response to injury/illness (e.g., level of consciousness, swelling, discoloration, warmth).

4. Signs and symptoms of athletic injuries/illnesses (e.g., crepitus, pain, discoloration, warmth).

Human Anatomy
5. Pathomechanics of athletic injury.

Human Physiology
6. Pathomechanics of athletic injury.

7. The body's immediate and delayed physiological response to injury/illness (e.g., level of consciousness, swelling, discoloration, warmth).

8. Signs and symptoms of athletic injuries/illnesses (e.g., crepitus, pain, discoloration, warmth).

Biomechanics
9. Pathomechanics of athletic injury.

10. Analysis of athletic activities.

11. Relationship between predisposing factors and athletic injuries/illnesses.

Nutrition
12. The consequences of inadequate fluid and electrolyte replacement.

Organization and Administration
13. Communication techniques in order to elicit information.

14. Medical terminology and standard nomenclature of athletic injuries/illnesses.

Skill in:

Domain-Specific Content
1. Identifying the extent and severity of athletic injuries/illnesses.

2. Observing the injury/illness scene.

Athletic Training Evaluation
3. Observing the injury/illness scene.

4. Recognizing athletic injuries/illnesses.

5. Identifying the extent and severity of athletic injuries/illnesses.

6. Obtaining signs and symptoms of specific athletic injuries/illnesses.

7. Relating predisposing factors to specific athletic injuries/illnesses.

8. Identifying anatomical structures involved in athletic injuries/illnesses.

Human Physiology
9. Assessing the body's pathological response of injury to homeostasis.

Nutrition
10. Identifying the signs and symptoms of fluid and electrolyte loss.

Organization and Administration
11. Relating signs and symptoms to specific athletic injuries/illnesses.

12. Recording information relating to the athletic injury/illness.

Task 2. Inspect the involved area using bilateral comparison, if appropriate, in order to determine the extent of the injury/illness.

Knowledge of:

Human Anatomy
1. Bony landmarks and soft tissue.

2. Circulatory system, nervous system, digestive system, muscular system, and skeletal system.

Human Physiology

3. Signs and symptoms (e.g., deformity, discoloration, bleeding) of athletic injuries/illnesses.

4. Response to injury/illness (e.g., pupils, shock, inflammation, bleeding).

5. Circulatory system, nervous system, digestive system, muscular system, and skeletal system.

Biomechanics

6. Normal and abnormal structural relationships as they relate to the pathomechanics of athletic injuries (e.g., valgus knees, varus forefoot, Q angle).

Athletic Training Evaluation

7. Normal and abnormal structural relationships as they relate to the pathomechanics of athletic injuries (e.g., valgus knees, varus forefoot, Q angle).

Organization and Administration

8. Medical terminology and standard nomenclature of athletic injuries/illnesses.

Skill in:

Domain-Specific Content

1. Removing athlete's equipment or clothing in order to recognize and evaluate injured area.

Human Physiology

2. Assessing the body's immediate and delayed physiological responses to injury/illness.

Biomechanics

3. Assessing pre-existing structural abnormalities and relating them to pathomechanics of injuries.

Athletic Training Evaluation

4. Recognizing the relationships and severity of pathological signs of athletic injuries/illnesses.

5. Identifying abnormalities of bony landmarks and soft tissue of specific injuries/illnesses.

Task 3. Palpate the involved area using knowledge of human anatomy in order to determine the extent of the injury/illness.

Knowledge of:

Human Anatomy
1. Musculoskeletal system with emphasis on bony landmarks and soft tissue structure.

Human Physiology
2. Body's immediate and delayed physiological response to injury/illness.

Skill in:

Human Anatomy
1. Locating and palpating bony landmarks, articulations, ligamentous structures, musculotendinous units, and other soft tissue.

Athletic Training Evaluation
2. Recognizing severity of pathological signs and symptoms of athletic injuries (e.g., internal and external).

3. Assessing body's immediate and delayed physiological response to injury.

4. Palpating pertinent areas of the body in order to assess integrity of human anatomical/physiological systems (e.g., circulatory, nervous, digestive, lymphatic).

Task 4. Perform specific tests on the involved area drawing on knowledge of anatomy, physiology, biomechanics, etc., in order to determine the extent of the injury/illness.

Knowledge of:

Domain-Specific Content
1. Specific sport and/or position requirements relative to the return to activity.

2. The importance of bilateral comparison.

Human Anatomy
3. Pathomechanics of injury.

Human Physiology
4. The body's immediate and delayed physiological response to injury.

Exercise Physiology
5. Signs and symptoms of systemic (i.e., cardiovascular, renal) requirements and failure during exercise.

Biomechanics
6. Pathomechanics of athletic injury.

Athletic Training Evaluation
7. Principles and techniques of assessing ROM, muscular strength or weakness, structural integrity, and functional capacity.

8. Specific tests for ROM, muscular strength or weakness, structural integrity, and functional capacity.

9. Interpreting information gained from specific tasks.

10. Sensory tests.

11. Motor tests.

12. Ligament tests.

13. Neurological tests.

14. Signs and symptoms of athletic injuries.

Organization and Administration
15. Medical terminology and standard nomenclature related to testing.

Skill in:

Athletic Training Evaluation
1. Assessing muscular strength by use of manual and/or mechanical muscle tests.

2. Assessing joint range of motion using test and measurement techniques.

3. Identifying the location and function of supportive ligamentous and musculotendinous structures.

4. Performing special tests.

5. Evaluating the information gained from tests.

6. Assessing neurological sensory and motor function.

7. Interpreting neurological and motor functional tests.

Exercise Physiology
8. Identifying the signs and symptoms of the body's systemic systems.

Biomechanics
9. Identifying location, type, function, and action of each joint.

Task 5. Determine the appropriate course of action by interpreting the signs and symptoms of the injury/illness in order to provide the necessary immediate care.

Knowledge of:

Domain-Specific Content
1. Appropriate first aid procedures.

Human Physiology
2. Signs and symptoms (e.g., temperature, blood pressure, nausea).

Pharmacology
3. The indications and contraindications for the use of prescription and non-prescription medication in the immediate care of athletic injuries and illnesses.

Organization and Administration
4. Scope of practice of other health care professionals.

5. Emergency management and referral systems.

Skill in:

Domain-Specific Content
1. Implementing appropriate treatment or referral to other medical personnel based on the body's response to pathological anomaly.

Athletic Training Evaluation
2. Assessing the body's response to pathological anomaly.

Nutrition

3. The replacement of fluids and electrolytes.

4. Determining an athlete's readiness to return to activity.

Organization and Administration

5. Efficient management in referral to other health care professionals.

Task 6. Administer first aid using standard, approved techniques and activate the emergency plan, if appropriate, in order to provide necessary medical care.

Knowledge of :

Domain-Specific Content

1. Current standards of first aid.

2. Current standards of cardiopulmonary resuscitation.

3. The methods for summoning emergency medical personnel.

4. The components of an emergency medical plan.

Human Anatomy

5. Effects of acute injury/illness.

Human Physiology

6. Effects of acute injury/illness.

Psychology/Counseling

7. Effects of acute injury/illness.

8. Counseling strategies.

Organization and Administration

9. Medical referral techniques.

10. Techniques for communicating with other health care professionals.

11. Proper communication with appropriate family members/athletic authorities (e.g., coaches, officials, administrators).

Skill in:

Domain-Specific Content
1. Administering current standards of first aid.

2. Administering current standards of cardiopulmonary resuscitation.

3. Implementing emergency medical plan.

Organization and Administration
4. Interpersonal communication with the acutely injured/ill athlete.

5. Communicating with health care professionals.

6. Communicating with appropriate family members, coaches, staff, etc.

Task 7. Select and apply emergency equipment following standard, approved techniques in order to facilitate the athlete or physically active individual's safe, proper, and efficient transportation.

Knowledge of:

Domain-Specific Content
1. Current first aid procedures.

2. Basic first aid equipment/supplies.

3. Emergency first aid equipment/supplies.

4. Safe and efficient transport of the injured/ill athlete or physically active individual.

Skill in:

Domain-Specific Content
1. Proper selection of basic emergency first aid equipment/supplies.

2. Proper application of basic emergency first aid equipment/supplies.

3. The maintenance of basic emergency first aid equipment/supplies.

4. Proper selection of transportation methods.

Organization and Administration

5. Controlling an acute athletic injury/illness scene.

6. Coordinating assisting personnel.

Task 8. Refer the athlete or physically active individual to the appropriate medical personnel and/or facility using standard procedures to continue proper medical care.

Knowledge of:

Organization and Administration

1. The role of various health care professionals relative to the medical evaluation/diagnosis and treatment of the injured/ill athlete or physically active individual.

2. Capabilities and availability of medical facilities.

3. Procedures (verbal and/or written) required for referral.

4. Procedures for referral of a minor.

Skill in:

Organization and Administration

1. Communicating with health care professionals.

2. Collecting information for continued care and documentation.

Domain 3. Rehabilitation and Reconditioning of Athletic Injuries

Task Evaluation

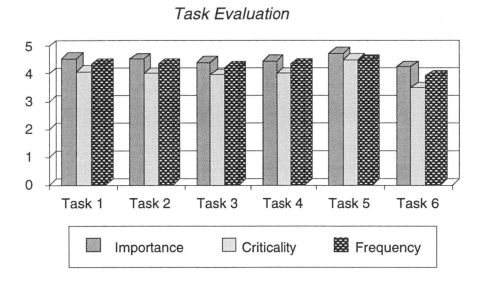

Evaluation and Allocation of Questions for Domain 3.

Task #	Importance Average	Criticality Average	Frequency Average	# Questions
1	4.55	4.07	4.33	7
2	4.52	4.01	4.33	7
3	4.41	3.96	4.23	7
4	4.46	4.01	4.34	7
5	4.73	4.49	4.47	9
6	4.24	3.49	3.92	5

Total number of questions from this domain on the examination: 42

Domain 3. Rehabilitation and Reconditioning of Athletic Injuries

Task 1. Identify injury/illness status by using standard techniques for evaluation and re-assessment in order to determine appropriate rehabilitation programs.

Knowledge of:

Athletic Training Evaluation
1. The signs and symptoms of the body's physiological response to trauma.

2. Evaluation techniques (e.g., inspection, palpation, special tests) to set the rehabilitation goals.

3. Evaluation techniques (e.g., inspection, palpation, special tests) to determine the athlete or physically active individual's response to the rehabilitation program.

4. Functional tests and measurements necessary to measure the athlete or physically active individual's progress through the rehabilitation program.

Human Anatomy
5. Normal and abnormal structural relationships related to mechanisms of athletic injury.

6. The current stage of rehabilitation.

Human Physiology
7. The current stage of rehabilitation.

8. The clinical and functional signs of tissue healing.

Exercise Physiology
9. The current stage of rehabilitation.

Biomechanics
10. Normal and abnormal structural relationships as they relate to mechanisms of athletic injury.

11. The biomechanical demands specific to athletic competition.

Nutrition
12. The current stage of rehabilitation.

Organization and Administration
13. Medical terminology and nomenclature.

14. Communicating rehabilitation plan and progress to the appropriate individuals.

Skill in:

Domain-Specific Content
1. Recognizing physiological response to therapeutic modalities.

2. Determining and adjusting short- and long-term goals with respect to the athlete or physically active individual's injury status.

Athletic Training Evaluation
3. Performing the techniques necessary to determine the athlete or physically active individual's current state in the healing process.

4. Recognizing the signs and symptoms of the physiological response to healing.

Task 2. Construct rehabilitation/re-conditioning programs for the injured/ill athlete or physically active individual using standard procedures for therapeutic exercise and modalities in order to restore functional status.

Knowledge of:

Domain-Specific Content
1. Theory and application modalities and the application in rehabilitation.

2. Theory and application of therapeutic exercise and the application in rehabilitation.

3. Functional tests and measurement techniques.

4. Therapeutic exercise equipment, techniques, and principles.

5. Specific rehabilitation protocols.

6. Indications and contraindications of therapeutic modalities.

7. Effects and possible adverse reactions to therapeutic modalities.

8. Indications and contraindications of therapeutic exercise.

9. The demands of sport and physical activity.

10. Manual therapy and its application in rehabilitation (e.g., massage, joint mobilization).

11. Surgical implications in rehabilitation and function.

Athletic Training Evaluation
12. The body's physiologic response to trauma, injury or illness, and healing.

Skill in:

Domain-Specific Content
1. Designing rehabilitation programs.

2. Evaluating rehabilitation programs.

Task 3. Select appropriate rehabilitation equipment, manual techniques, and therapeutic modalities by evaluating the theory and use as defined by accepted standards of care in order to enhance recovery.

Knowledge of:

Domain-Specific Content
1. The principles of isometric, isotonic, and isokinetic exercise.

2. The effects of electricity on the muscular, skeletal, circulatory, and nervous systems.

3. The therapeutic modalities (e.g., exercise, heat, cold, electricity) on soft tissue injuries or other injuries.

4. The indications and contraindications of rehabilitation equipment and therapeutic modalities.

5. The set up and operation of therapeutic modalities and exercise equipment.

6. Principles of manual techniques (e.g., soft tissue techniques, joint mobilization).

7. Indications and contraindications of exercise as they relate to specific injuries.

Human Physiology
8. Effects of electricity, sound, and heat on tissues of the human body.

Exercise Physiology

9. Effects of active resistance and passive exercise on tissues of the human body.

10. Indications and contraindications of exercise.

Physics

11. Electrical theory as it relates to electrotherapeutic modalities (e.g., volts, currents, wave forms).

12. The principles of physics as they relate to the design, content, etc., of rehabilitative exercise equipment (e.g., levers, forces).

13. Transmission of heat.

14. Principles and characteristics of sound.

Skill in:

Domain-Specific Content

1. Selecting and applying rehabilitative equipment.

2. Selecting and applying therapeutic modalities.

3. Selecting and applying manual techniques.

4. Selecting and applying therapeutic exercise.

5. Evaluating literature on the theory of operation of rehabilitative equipment, exercise, manual techniques, and therapeutic modalities.

6. Interpreting the results of isokinetic testing.

Task 4. Administer rehabilitation techniques and procedures to the injured/ill athlete or physically active individual by applying accepted standards of care and protocols in order to enhance recovery.

Knowledge of:

Domain-Specific Content

1. Wrapping and bracing procedures.

2. Therapeutic modalities including application and physiological effects.

3. Therapeutic exercise and procedures including application and physiological effects.

4. Proper use of ambulatory aids and devices designed to protect/support an injured part.

5. Administering rehabilitation techniques and procedures.

Athletic Training Evaluation
6. Assessment procedures (e.g., functional, ROM, and muscle testing).

Human Physiology
7. The body's immediate and delayed response to injury or illness.

Exercise Physiology
8. The body's adaptation to exercise.

Psychology/Counseling
9. Immediate and delayed response to injury or illness.

Pharmacology
10. Prescription and non-prescription pharmacological agents used in the care and treatment of athletic injuries/illnesses.

11. The dispensing or administration of prescription and non-prescription medications.

12. The indications and contraindications of prescription and non-prescription medications.

13. Reactions and adverse reactions of prescription and non-prescription medications.

Skill in:

Domain-Specific Content
1. The recognition of the physiological/psychological responses to trauma, healing, and exercise.

2. The use of therapeutic modalities (e.g., cold, heat, water, sound, electricity, massage).

3. The application of therapeutic exercises (e.g., manual isokinetic, closed chain).

4. The fit and use of ambulatory aids and protective devices.

5. The application and fabrication of wrapping and bracing procedures.

6. The application of manual therapy techniques.

Athletic Training Evaluation
7. Regularly evaluating the injured/ill athlete or physically active individual for the purpose of monitoring response to treatment.

Human Physiology
8. Recognizing the physiological responses to trauma, healing, and exercise.

Psychology/Counseling
9. Recognizing the psychological responses to trauma, healing, and exercise.

10. Motivating an individual to execute a rehabilitation program.

Task 5. Evaluate the readiness of the injured/ill athlete or physically active individual by assessing functional status in order to ensure a safe return to participation.

Knowledge of:

Domain-Specific Content
1. Criteria for return to sport or activities (e.g., strength, ROM, flexibility, sport-specific tests).

2. Sport or activity to which the athlete or physically active individual will return.

Athletic Training Evaluation
3. Information gained from specific tests used to determine functional status.

4. Functional testing principles and techniques.

Exercise Physiology
5. Level of cardiovascular fitness required for specific physical activity.

6. Level of neuromuscular fitness (e.g., muscular, strength, proprioception, kinesthesia, flexibility) required for specific activities.

Psychology/Counseling
7. Psychological readiness to return to participation.

Skill in:

Domain-Specific Content
1. Analyzing information gained from test of functional status.

2. Evaluating information gained from strength, ROM, flexibility, and endurance tests.

Athletic Training Evaluation
3. Developing tests to determine functional status.

4. Evaluating tests for determining functional status.

Exercise Physiology
5. Testing neuromuscular (fitness, strength, proprioception, kinesthesia, flexibility) fitness.

Psychology/Counseling
6. Evaluating psychological readiness.

Task 6. Educate parents, staff, coaches, athletes, physically active individuals, etc. about the rehabilitation process using direct communication in order to enhance rehabilitation.

Knowledge of:

Psychology/Counseling
1. Interpersonal communication skills needed to disseminate appropriate rehabilitation information.

Skill in:

Domain-Specific Content
1. Instructing the athlete or physically active individual in the use of therapeutic exercise equipment.

2. Instructing the athlete or physically active individual in therapeutic exercise regimen.

Domain 4. Health Care Administration

Task Evaluation

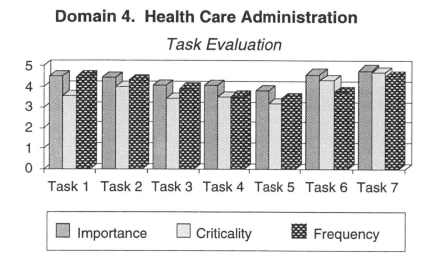

Evaluation and Allocation of Questions for Domain 4

Task #	Importance Average	Criticality Average	Frequency Average	# Questions
1	4.49	3.57	4.47	1
2	4.44	3.98	4.30	2
3	4.07	3.42	3.90	1
4	4.06	3.47	3.52	1
5	3.81	3.15	3.42	1
6	4.60	4.33	3.74	1
7	4.80	4.68	4.51	2

Total number of questions from this domain on the examination: 9

Domain 4. Health Care Administration

Task 1. Maintain the health care records of the athlete or physically active individual using a recognized, comprehensive recording process in order to document procedures/services rendered by health care professionals.

Knowledge of:

Pharmacology
1. The proper maintenance and documentation of records for the administration of prescription and non-prescription medication.

2. Laws and regulations governing the storage and dispensing of prescription and non-prescription medications.

Organization and Administration
3. The subjective, objective, assessment, and plan (SOAP) of data collection.

4. Standard medical nomenclature.

5. The required content of a medical record.

6. Information systems as applied to data collection and analysis (written, computerized).

7. The legal responsibilities regarding confidentiality of the medical record and consent for treatment.

Skill in:

Pharmacology
1. The maintenance and documentation of records for the administration of prescription and non-prescription medication.

Organization and Administration
2. Creating and completing the documentation process of medical record keeping including the components of SOAP notes.

3. Utilizing proper medical terminology.

4. Constructing and compiling the medical record.

5. Obtaining written authorization for treatment and release of medical information.

6. Demonstrating effective communication.

Task 2. Comply with safety and sanitation standards by maintaining facilities and equipment in order to ensure a safe environment.

Knowledge of:

Organization and Administration

1. Federal, state, and/or other applicable sanitation standards for health care facilities, equipment, and therapeutic modalities (National Fire Protection Agency Codes, Joint Commission on Accreditation of Hospital Standards, etc.).

2. Institutional procedures for maintenance of facilities.

3. Legal documentation requirements of JCAHO, OSHA, etc.

4. Universal precautions required in managing infectious diseases.

5. Safety standards (e.g., fire, hazardous chemicals, severe weather, evacuation) for facilities.

6. Safety maintenance standards and requirements for equipment.

Skill in:

Organization and Administration

1. Evaluating facility for potential hazards and risks.

2. Implementing institutional policies and procedures for the maintenance of facilities, equipment, and therapeutic modalities.

3. Proper containment and disposal of biohazardous waste.

Task 3. Manage daily operations by implementing and maintaining standards for all personnel in order to ensure quality of service.

Knowledge of:

Organization and Administration

1. How to develop a job description and performance appraisal.

2. Organizational structure and hierarchy.

3. Specific job responsibilities of personnel in the department.

4. Information systems related to department policies and procedures.

5. Mandated drug-testing procedures and department protocols.

6. Legal standards defining negligence.

Skill in:

Psychology/Counseling
1. Problem-solving techniques.

Organization and Administration
2. Recognizing and defining job roles and responsibilities.

3. Evaluating job performance through interpersonal communication throughout the department.

4. Planning staff work loads and operating hours of the department.

Task 4. Establish written guidelines for injury/illness management by standardizing operating procedures in order to provide a consistent quality of care.

Knowledge of:

Organization and Administration
1. Components of policy and procedural guidelines.

2. Organizational structures.

3. Mechanisms ensuring quality of care.

4. Applicable laws.

Skill in:

Organization and Administration
1. Obtaining and interpreting information.

2. Determining relevance and appropriateness of policies and procedures.

3. Effective verbal and written communication.

4. Formulating policy and procedural guidelines.

Task 5. Obtain equipment and supplies by evaluating reliable product information in order to provide athletic training services for athletes and physically active individuals.

Knowledge of:

Organization and Administration
1. Purchasing practices, including determination of needs, selection of items, bid letting, and inventory control.

2. Financial principles in areas of budgeting and purchasing.

Skill in:

Organization and Administration
1. Evaluating equipment and supply requirements.

2. Writing equipment supply orders.

3. Instructing on the proper utilization of equipment or supplies.

4. Evaluating equipment to determine effectiveness.

5. Implementing an inventory control system.

Task 6. Create a plan which includes emergency, management, and referral systems specific to the setting by involving appropriate health care professionals in order to facilitate proper care.

Knowledge of:

Athletic Training Evaluation
1. Signs and symptoms necessitating referral to other health care professionals.

2. Situations requiring consultation with professionals.

3. The athlete or physically active individual's physical, social, cultural, and/or personal issues.

Nutrition

4. Roles and responsibilities of other health care professionals in the referral process.

5. Personal and community health issues.

Organization and Administration

6. Components of local and emergency support services.

7. Regional statutes related to emergency care services.

8. Department or institution's communication systems.

9. Specific requirements to activate EMS.

10. Local/regional health care delivery systems, hospitals, doctors, and insurance guidelines.

Skill in:

Athletic Training Evaluation

1. Recognizing signs and symptoms of injury.

Psychology/Counseling

2. Identifying signs and symptoms of emotional, behavioral, and physical status.

3. Identifying signs and symptoms of unhealthy personal behavior.

4. Assisting in intervention as directed by appropriate health care professionals.

5. Making referrals to the appropriate health care provider.

Nutrition

6. Making referrals to the appropriate health care provider.

Organization and Administration

7. Effectively communicating with local emergency personnel, physicians, parents, and various types of insurance options.

8. Evaluating medical triage operations.

9. Systematic decision making relating to the injury disposition.

Task 7. Reduce the risk of exposure to infectious agents by following universal precautions in order to prevent the transmission of infectious diseases.

Knowledge of:

Organization and Administration
1. Universal precautions.

2. Transmission of infectious agents.

3. Risk of exposure to infection.

4. Federal, state, and other applicable infection control standards.

Skill in:

Organization and Administration
1. Determining the necessity for and use of personal protective equipment.

2. Implementing the procedures with universal precautions.

Domain 5. Professional Development and Responsibility

Task Evaluation

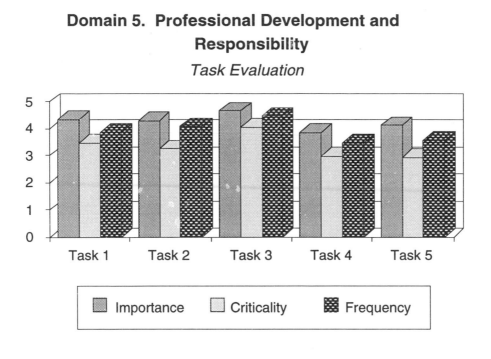

| Importance | Criticality | Frequency |

Evaluation and Allocation of Questions for Domain 5

Task #	Importance Average	Criticality Average	Frequency Average	# Questions
1	4.35	3.46	3.85	2
2	4.28	3.24	4.08	2
3	4.66	4.04	4.47	3
4	3.87	2.97	3.46	1
5	4.13	2.94	3.56	1

Total number of questions from this domain on the examination: 9

Domain 5. Professional Development and Responsibility

Task 1. Maintain knowledge of contemporary sports medicine issues by participating in continuing education activities in order to provide an appropriate standard of care.

Knowledge of:

Domain-Specific Content
1. Resources for current information about contemporary sports medicine issues.

2. NATABOC continuing education requirements (CEUs).

3. Continuing education resources (e.g., workshops, seminars, clinics, materials).

Skill in:

Domain-Specific Content
1. Demonstrating newly developed athletic training techniques.

2. Recognizing and communicating to the athlete or physically active individual the purpose or need for professional consultation outside of the sports medicine profession.

3. Explaining data regarding athletic injuries and the potential futuristic impact.

4. Obtaining and recording information related to athletic health issues.

5. Evaluating literature on the theories of current sports medicine issues.

Task 2. Develop interpersonal communication skills by interacting with others (e.g., parents, coaches, colleagues, athletes, physically active individuals) in order to enhance proficiency and professionalism.

Knowledge of:

Psychology/Counseling
1. Motivational techniques and group dynamics as they relate to interpersonal communication.

2. Theories and techniques of interpersonal communication.

3. Instructional techniques for interpersonal communication skills.

4. Communication techniques in order to elicit information.

Organization and Administration
5. Proper communication with appropriate family members and/or athletic authorities (e.g., coaches, officials, administrators).

6. Techniques for communicating with other emergency medical personnel.

7. Computer operations and software as applied to developing communications among health care professionals.

Skill in:

Organization and Administration
1. Communicating with medical and/or paramedical personnel.

2. Communicating with appropriate family members and/or athletic authorities.

3. Communicating with health care professionals regarding the care and treatment of the injured/ill athlete or physically active individual.

4. Instructing the athlete or physically active individual in the use of therapeutic exercise equipment.

5. Instructing athletes, physically active individuals, and student trainers how to complete forms.

6. Computer operations and programming as they affect communication.

7. Communicating with appropriate facility personnel.

8. Collaborating in both verbal and written form with personnel involved with emergency medical services.

9. Interacting with the athlete or physically active individual in all situations.

10. Interacting with athletic staff, health professionals, athletic training staff, and other involved persons.

11. Recognizing confidential communication.

Task 3. **Adhere to ethical and legal parameters by following established guidelines which define the proper role of the certified athletic trainer in order to protect athletes, physically active individuals, and the public.**

Knowledge of:

Domain-Specific Content
1. The NATABOC Code of Professional Practice.

2. State regulations.

3. State statutes that regulate other professional organizations that interface with the athletic training profession.

4. Ethical and legal parameters.

5. The insurance claim system.

Skill in:

Domain-Specific Content
1. Proper legal and ethical conduct.

2. Recognizing confidential information.

Task 4. **Assimilate appropriate sports medicine research by using available resources in order to enhance professional growth.**

Knowledge of:

Domain-Specific Content
1. Principles of collecting and processing data.

2. Data analysis.

3. Types of computers and software.

4. Current and pertinent research in athletic injury or illness.

Skill in:

Domain-Specific Content
1. Recognizing need for information regarding personal and/or community health topics.

2. Evaluating literature pertinent to the practice of athletic training.

3. Assessing the validity and reliability of research.

4. Interpreting data.

Task 5. Educate the public by serving as a resource in order to enhance awareness of the roles and responsibilities of the certified athletic trainer.

Knowledge of:

Organization and Administration
1. Methods of disseminating information to the general public.

2. Needs relating to athletic health care.

Skill in:

Organization and Administration
1. Interacting with the general public.

2. Assessing the needs of the community regarding athletic training.

Performance Domains

Knowledge and skills particular to each performance domain

Universal Competencies / Domain-Specific Content	Prevention of Athletic Injuries	Recognition, Evaluation, and Immediate Care of Athletic Injuries	Rehabilitation and Reconditioning of Athletic Injuries	Health Care Administration	Professional Development and Responsibility
Athletic Training Evaluation	Determination of an athlete's physical readiness to participate.	Identification of underlying trauma.	Ongoing evaluation of an athlete's progress through various stages of rehabilitation.	Documentation of injury status and rehabilitation.	Remains up-to-date with current evaluation skills, techniques and knowledge.
Human Anatomy	Normal anatomical structure and function.	Recognition of signs and symptoms of athletic injury and illness.	Normal anatomical structure and function.		Remains up-to-date in current human anatomical research and trends.
Human Physiology	Normal physiological function.	Recognition of signs and symptoms of athletic injury and illness.	Stages of injury response.		Remains up-to-date in current human physiology research and trends.
Exercise Physiology	Physiological demand and response to exercise.	Recognition of systemic and local metabolic failure.	Musculoskeletal and cardiovascular demands placed on the injured athlete.		Remains up-to-date with current exercise physiology research and trends.
Biomechanics	Normal biomechanical demands of exercise.	Identification of pathomechanics.	Resolution of pathomechanical motion.		Remains up-to-date with current biomechanical research and trends.
Psychology/ Counseling	Educational program for the healthy and injured athlete (i.e., alcohol and other drug abuse, performance anxiety).	Recognition of the psychological signs and symptoms of athletic injury and illness.	Psychological implications of injury.	Communication with, and referral to, the appropriate health care provider.	Continues to develop interpersonal and communication skills.
Nutrition	Nutritional demands of the athlete.	Recognition of the effects of improper nutritional needs of the competing athlete (i.e., fluid replacement, diabetic shock).	Nutritional demands placed on the injured athlete.	Referral to the appropriate health care provider.	Remains up-to-date with current nutritional research and trends.
Pharmacology	Contraindications and side effects of prescription and non-prescription medications.	The role of prescription and non-prescription medication in the immediate/emergency care of athletic injury and illness.	The role of prescription and non-prescription medications in the stages of injury response.	Proper maintenance and documentation of records for the administration of prescription and non-prescription medication.	Remains up-to-date with current pharmacological research and trends.
Physics	Absorption, dissipation, and transmission of energy of varying materials.	The effect of stress loads on the human body (i.e., shear, tensile, compressive forces).	Physiological response to various energies imposed on the body.		Remains up-to-date with current knowledge of physics as it relates to athletic training.
Organization and Administration	Legal requirements and rules of the sport.	Planning, documentation, and communication of appropriate rehabilitation strategies to the necessary parties.	Planning, documentation, and communication of appropriate rehabilitation strategies to the necessary parties.	Development of operational policies and procedures.	Remains up-to-date with current standards of professional practice.

Appendix 2. Importance and Criticality Rating Scales

Importance: How important each performance domain is to the performance of an entry-level certified athletic trainer.

> *1 = Not Important:* Performance of tasks in this domain is not essential to the job performance of the entry-level certified athletic trainer.

> *2 = Somewhat Important:* Performance of tasks in this domain is minimally essential to the job performance of the entry-level certified athletic trainer.

> *3 = Important:* Performance of tasks in this domain is moderately essential to the job performance of the entry-level certified athletic trainer.

> *4 = Very Important:* Performance of tasks in this domain is clearly essential to the job performance of the entry-level certified athletic trainer.

> *5 = Extremely Important:* Performance of tasks in this domain is absolutely essential to the job performance of the entry-level certified athletic trainer.

Criticality: The degree to which inability to perform tasks in each performance domain would be seen as causing harm to an athlete or physically active individual, an athletic trainer, a clinic, the public, etc. Harm may be physical, emotional, or financial.

> *1 = No Harm:* Inability to perform tasks in this domain would have no adverse consequences.

> *2 = Minimal Harm:* Inability to perform tasks in this domain would lead to error with minimal adverse consequences.

> *3 = Moderate Harm:* Inability to perform tasks in this domain would lead to error with moderate adverse consequences.

> *4 = Significant Harm:* Inability to perform tasks in this domain would lead to error with major adverse consequences.

> *5 = Extreme Harm:* Inability to perform tasks in this domain would definitely lead to error with severe consequences.

Frequency: The percentage of time spent by entry-level certified athletic trainers in performing duties associated with the domains and tasks.

Appendix 3. Domains and Tasks

Domain 1. Prevention of Athletic Injuries

Task 1. Identify physical conditions predisposing the athlete or physically active individual to increased risk of injury/illness in athletic activity by following accepted pre-participation examination guidelines in order to ensure safe participation.

Task 2. Supervise conditioning programs and testing for athletes or physically active individuals using mechanical and/or other techniques in order to ensure readiness for safe participation in physical activity.

Task 3. Monitor environmental conditions (e.g., temperature, humidity, lightning) of playing or practice areas by following accepted guidelines in order to make recommendations regarding safe participation.

Task 4. Assess athletic apparatuses and athletic activity areas (e.g., playing surfaces, gyms, locker and athletic training room facilities) by periodic inspection and review of maintenance records to ensure a safe environment.

Task 5. Construct custom protective devices by fabricating and fitting with appropriate materials in order to protect specific parts of the body from injury during athletic activity.

Task 6. Apply specific and appropriate taping, wrapping, or prophylactic devices to the athlete or physically active individual by adhering to principles of biomechanics and injury mechanism in order to prevent injury or re-injury.

Task 7. Evaluate the use and maintenance of protective devices and athletic equipment (e.g., helmets, shoulder pads, shin guards) by inspecting and assessing the equipment in order to ensure optimal protection of the athlete or physically active individual.

Task 8. Educate parents, staff, coaches, athletes, etc., about the risks associated with participation and unsafe practices using direct communication in order to provide an opportunity for them to make an informed decision concerning physical activity.

Domain 2. Recognition, Evaluation, and Immediate Care of Athletic Injuries

Task 1. Obtain a history from the athlete or physically active individual or witnesses through observation and interview in order to determine the pathology and extent of injury/illness.

Task 2. Inspect the involved area using bilateral comparison, if appropriate, in order to determine the extent of the injury/illness.

Task 3. Palpate the involved area using knowledge of human anatomy in order to determine the extent of the injury/illness.

Task 4. Perform specific tests on the involved area drawing on knowledge of anatomy, physiology, biomechanics, etc., in order to determine the extent of the injury/illness.

Task 5. Determine the appropriate course of action by interpreting the signs and symptoms of the injury/illness in order to provide the necessary immediate care.

Task 6. Administer first aid using standard, approved techniques and activate the emergency plan, if appropriate, in order to provide necessary medical care.

Task 7. Select and apply emergency equipment following standard, approved techniques in order to facilitate the athlete or physically active individual's safe, proper, and efficient transportation.

Task 8. Refer the athlete or physically active individual to the appropriate medical personnel and/or facility using standard procedures to continue proper medical care.

Domain 3. Rehabilitation and Reconditioning of Athletic Injuries

Task 1. Identify injury/illness status by using standard techniques for evaluation and re-assessment in order to determine appropriate rehabilitation programs.

Task 2. Construct rehabilitation/re-conditioning programs for the injured/ill athlete or physically active individual using standard procedures for therapeutic exercise and modalities in order to restore functional status.

Task 3. Select appropriate rehabilitation equipment, manual techniques, and therapeutic modalities by evaluating the theory and use as defined by accepted standards of care in order to enhance recovery.

Task 4. Administer rehabilitation techniques and procedures to the injured/ill athlete or physically active individual by applying accepted standards of care and protocols in order to enhance recovery.

Task 5. Evaluate the readiness of the injured/ill athlete or physically active individual by assessing functional status in order to ensure a safe return to participation.

Task 6. Educate parents, staff, coaches, athletes, physically active individuals, etc., about the rehabilitation process using direct communication in order to enhance rehabilitation.

Domain 4. Health Care Administration

Task 1. Maintain the health care records of the athlete or physically active individual using a recognized, comprehensive recording process in order to document procedures/services rendered by health care professionals.

Task 2. Comply with safety and sanitation standards by maintaining facilities and equipment in order to ensure a safe environment.

Task 3. Manage daily operations by implementing and maintaining standards for all personnel in order to ensure quality of service.

Task 4. Establish written guidelines for injury/illness management by standardizing operating procedures in order to provide a consistent quality of care.

Task 5. Obtain equipment and supplies by evaluating reliable product information in order to provide athletic training services for athletes and physically active individuals.

Task 6. Create a plan which includes emergency, management, and referral systems specific to the setting by involving appropriate health care professionals in order to facilitate proper care.

Task 7. Reduce the risk of exposure to infectious agents by following universal precautions in order to prevent the transmission of infectious diseases.

Domain 5. Professional Development and Responsibility

Task 1. Maintain knowledge of contemporary sports medicine issues by participating in continuing education activities in order to provide an appropriate standard of care.

Task 2. Develop interpersonal communication skills by interacting with others (e.g., parents, coaches, colleagues, athletes, physically active individuals) in order to enhance proficiency and professionalism.

Task 3. Adhere to ethical and legal parameters by following established guidelines which define the proper role of the certified athletic trainer in order to protect athletes, physically active individuals, and the public.

Task 4. Assimilate appropriate sports medicine research by using available resources in order to enhance professional growth.

Task 5. Educate the public by serving as a resource in order to enhance awareness of the roles and responsibilities of the certified athletic trainer.